When Amelia gets mad, she doesn't feel like herself anymore.

She named her anger Angria.

For your own inner Angria

Text copyright © 2022 by Angelia Sterling

Illustrations copyright © 2022 by Greg Sterling

All rights reserved. Published by Silent i Publishing.

ISBN 978-1-952678-07-3 (pbk)

ISBN 978-1-952678-08-0 (hardcover)

ISBN 978-1-952678-09-7 (ebook)

Visit A.D. Sterling at www.adsterling.com

Special thanks to Joel Cardinal for his artistic direction

ANGRIA

Amelia Copes with Her Anger

by A.D. Sterling

Illustrated by Greg Sterling

Amelia woke up that morning feeling angry.

Everything from that moment on went wrong.

When Amelia pulled on her favorite rainbow tights, her foot ripped through the seam.

When Amelia put her hair into a pigtail, the hair tie broke and snapped her hand.

"Ouch!" yelped Angria.

On her way to the kitchen,
she tripped over the cat.

"Move, Muffins!" Angria cried.

Dad made toast with Amelia's favorite jam. It was cut into neat slices.

"I can't eat this!" Angria shouted.
"Dad, you know I only eat them if they're triangles!"

Amelia planted her feet firmly on the ground and held her arms stiff in the air.

"It's not working," Angria grunted.

School wasn't any better for Amelia.

Her best friend was out sick.
She didn't understand the math lesson,
and it was raining during recess.

"That's mine!" Angria yelled.

Amelia held the bear protectively. "Don't touch my stuff, Allen!"

That night, Amelia just wanted the day to be over.
She changed into her pajamas and put herself to bed early.

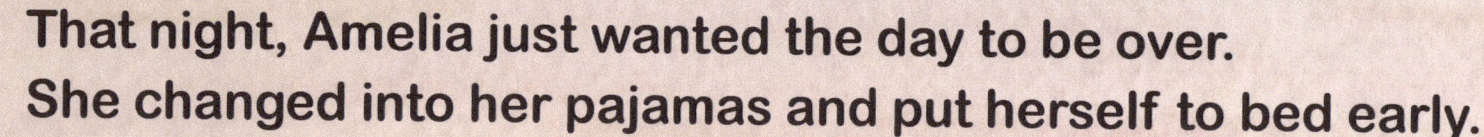

"And I was able to fix these," Mom said, handing Amelia her favorite rainbow tights.

"When you're having a bad day, sometimes it helps to look for the good things too. There must be at least one good thing that happened to you," said Mom.

"This is one," Amelia said, giving Mom a big hug.
"I'm sorry I was mean today. I don't want to be angry anymore."

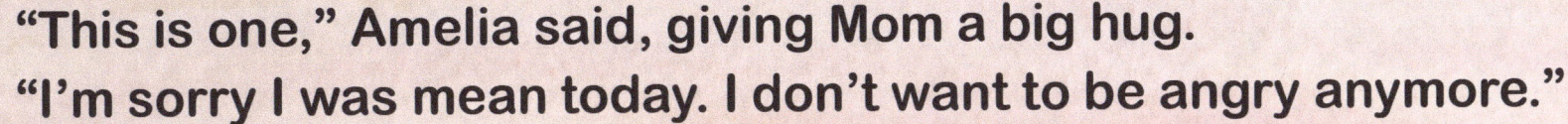

"When I feel mad, I try to stop what I'm doing, close my eyes, and take some big deep breaths."

Amelia sighed loudly.

"What's something that makes *you* feel better?" asked Mom.
"When you sing to me and rub my back," Amelia replied.

CPSIA information can be obtained
at www.ICGtesting.com
Printed in the USA
LVHW071905230323
742409LV00003B/112